DO LEADERSHIP

A Step by Step Guide to 'Doing' Thought Leadership
for Solopreneurs & Small Business Owners

Nicole Croizier, Laura B. Lorenz, Ray L. Perry, and
Kelly Weppler Hernandez

Do Leadership

www.ducttapepublishing.com

Praise for *Do Leadership*

"Anything that comes from the Duct Tape Marketing brand is solid gold. And, this book is no different. It's also an important book. Leadership is hard but without real leadership there are no sales, no effective marketing campaigns and no business development that makes a difference. Read this book. Your future depends on it."

Michael Port
NY Times, WSJ bestseller of *Book Yourself Solid* and *Steal the Show*

"While there are many self-appointed thought leaders among us today, we all know that true thought leadership is spoken through action - Do Leadership will teach you how to lead with insight and heart"

Carrie Wilkerson, The Barefoot Executive

"If you roll your eyes when you hear the term "thought leader", this book is for you. The authors of Do Leadership present thought leadership in hype-free and pragmatic terms, a hallmark of their Duct Tape Marketing pedigree. And the book exemplifies the principles it espouses: a unique perspective and authentic voice that make us perk up and pay attention. Plus, some parts are laugh-out-loud funny!"

Jon Hall, Founder & CEO Grade.us

"If you want to stand out in a crowded entrepreneurial field as a Small Business Owner and be seen as the most highly valued individual to do business with over your competition, then you want to recognized as the leader *in your niche. So how do you become that magnet, the one that attracts business over your competition verse wasting marketing dollars with little to no results? You know, the one that makes your competition jealous and stay up all night dreaming to be more like you? It all starts with "Doing" Thought Leadership and this is the book that shows you exactly how to do it, step-by-step and be that business your competitors fantasize of becoming one day."*

Mike Kawula, CEO Social Quant

"The era of the "Thought Leader" is over. If you want to rapidly grow your audience today, you need to be seen as an action leader. And Do Leadership is a step-by-step guide that will show you how to shift from "Thought Leader" to "Do Leader" in a matter of days. Highly recommended."

Brian Dean, Founder & CEO Backlinko

TABLE OF CONTENTS

FOREWORD

You might have the same reaction I typically have when I hear the term thought leader these day – that it's used and abused. But don't let that initial opinion prevent you from taking a much closer look at an idea that can truly revolutionize how you do business.

As a thought leader, you're NOT someone who pontificates on complicated concepts. On the contrary! As a thought leader, your job is to communicate your unique point of view and make the big ideas of your industry simpler and more understandable for the people who need to grasp them most – prospective users of your products and services.

The thing is a true thought leader simply does this – they don't talk about it, they don't anoint themselves with a title – some tribe or community somewhere determines that what they have to say and share is worth listening to and perhaps acting upon.

To take up this mantle you don't have to lock yourself away in an ivory tower to contemplate the intricacies of your industry – just allow your natural curiosity to lead you to keep learning and to convey what you learn to anyone who is listening.

Service is at the heart of thought leadership. You serve by providing valuable information and insight. You become the person people seek out when they need to find the real deal.

How do you do that? You're about to find out as you read Do Leadership, which was created by some of the finest Duct Tape Marketing Consultants I've had the privilege to mentor over the years. They took on an enormous task in dissecting and simplifying a concept that has been complicated to the point where it's nearly useless.

Quite simply, becoming a thought leader happens as you attract people who recognize you as someone worth listening to and following. Making this happen is not as difficult as it sounds, and as you read this book, you'll see what an important role content creation plays in building your credibility.

You'll also see how to make your authentic point of view - the unique message you bring to the marketplace – even if it's not earth shattering. Becoming a thought leader is not at all the same as winning some sort of popularity contest. In fact, it can be the exact opposite – but in the process of being who you are and taking your stand as a thought leader, you'll find that you attract the people you are best suited to serve. That's where the power of thought leadership comes in.

John Jantsch
Founder, Duct Tape Marketing

CHAPTER 1

WHY "DO" LEADERSHIP

*As Sriracha, Pho, and Kombucha are to foodies
and hipsters, thought leadership has become
the next new craze among marketers.*

Thought Leadership. You've heard the term – probably frequently enough that you've become deaf to it already. You may have even used the term – the same way we tentatively place an order at the food truck of an unfamiliar cuisine, hoping you're not about to be humiliated by someone pointing out that you've done it wrong.

Odds are, you've dismissed *thought leadership* from your vocabulary and your marketing strategy arsenal as well. It sounds like such an amorphous, billowy term – the kind that suggests you should already know what it means – that not knowing what it means seems like grounds for being removed from the cool kids' table. It also sounds like a fantastically effective marketing tactic – but for someone else, someone with a bigger company, a more prominent public presence, a more interesting product or service. Most definitely, thought leadership sounds like one of those fantastic ideas that turns out to be highly theoretical and nearly impossible for the average person to implement, one step down the intellectual ladder from grasping string theory.

But here's the truth...

All of those objections? Smoke and mirrors, the likes of which, if you were to have an arch nemesis marketing-wise, would be used to distract you and nudge you back into Me-Too Marketing Hell, where you're left with nothing but a spork and a bullet-ridden PowerPoint presentation to defend yourself. Your competitors are looking at thought leadership, and the first company in any niche that nails it takes home the booty – an endless stream of ideal, educated customers who refuse to do business with anyone but you.

The truth is, thought leadership is both easy to define and easy to understand. It's probably a stunningly perfect fit for your company. And as far as practicality goes, you're about to be surprised at how easy (and powerful) implementation can be.

You might have crossed thought leadership off of your list of "marketing stuff to master this year" – and yet, here you stand, holding this book. There's a good reason your eyes drew you to this book, and it's probably got something to do with *Thought* being crossed out and *DO* in big, bold print.

Why? Because you're Action Jackson. Well, minus the 1.5-star IMDb rating, the vengeance-driven maniacal action, and the hours of gratuitously violent Bollywood plot clichés. Other than that, it's good rhyming and it conveys the main point: thought leadership is all about DOING.

That sure sounds like you, doesn't it? You're all about learning what's working and then doing something about what you've learned.

That's what we like doing, too. Sure it's fun in a marketing geek sort of way to study algorithms, pore through case studies, and aggregate split test results. But what's really fun is sharing marketing strategies and tactics with business owners – or folks who are responsible for the marketing in their companies – and seeing them implement them and get the kind of results that make their eyebrows go up (well, at least the first time, until big numbers lose their shock value).

Maybe it's time for a quick introduction. We're a group of Certified and Master Consultants with the leading small business marketing brand, Duct Tape Marketing. Practicality is practically in our name – duct tape.

We work with small business owners every day to make marketing as simple, practical, effective, and straightforward as possible. One of the strategies we've identified for business owners as having the most potential to help them grow their businesses is thought leadership. It's a strategy that's too good not to share.

Just like everyone else who writes about thought leadership, we could hit you with page after page of dry, boring theory. We could drone on about the merits of this tactic until you begged for mercy, but we're about getting results – and that doesn't happen from theory.

That's why this book is *DO Leadership.* We wanted to provide a guide that's easy to read and even easier to implement – a step-by-step process for applying the theories behind thought leadership to real life. Talking and thinking about thought leadership is fine and dandy. DOING thought leadership is where it counts, and how it becomes your new favorite strategy for catapulting your business past your competitors.

Are you up for making a little pinky promise here? We promise not to bore you with theoretical pie in the sky discourse and instead give you actionable info you can use today – and you promise not to just think about thought leadership, but actually do it. Do we have a deal?

If so, a solid definition is in order. An article in *Forbes* nails the simplest definition we've seen for thought leadership:

*"Thought leadership is a way for a brand to position itself as a leader in a certain field or sector by **demonstrating** its values or expertise."*

There's a good reason *demonstrating* is in bold. Thought leadership doesn't happen by proclaiming yourself an expert or leader in your field. It happens by proving that you're an expert and a leader. At a practical level, this is accomplished by continually educating your audience – not just on your specific products or services, but also on your industry best practices and solutions to people's problems.

That's great news when you think about it. You're already doing expert stuff every single day your doors are open. You've solved more problems for more people (your customers) than you can count. You know the answers to your prospects' burning questions. And you likely have a unique point of view. Now all you've got to do is to communicate that expertise in a way that your prospects "get" and that leaves them convinced they'd be silly to go to your competitor instead.

In writing this book, we asked several thought leaders across different industries for their opinions on thought leadership and how they've used the concept in their own success. You'll find their comments highlighted throughout the book.

> *Thought leadership is really just somebody who is willing to be authentic and put themselves out there and express an opinion and see what other people have to say about it.*
>
> **Ed Kless, Radio Talk Show Host, Partner Department and Strategy for Sage Group**

You've got the hard part down – learning enough about your specialty to become an expert. Now you just have a little further to go to leverage that expertise, and:

- **Total market domination is within reach – well, on some level.**
  Very few small businesses are doing this at all, and, surprisingly, very few medium-large sized businesses are doing it well.

- **You can think and act rather than spend big money.**
  The investment in this process is more in time, strategy, and energy vs. money.

- **Your thought leadership accumulates and lasts, unlike buying advertisements.**
  This is an incremental strategy, where the educational content you share continues to work for you over time, as compared to paid tactics like advertising that go away quickly.

- **You can kiss selling goodbye.**
  The continual process of educating your audience reduces the need to sell. In many cases, you get what we call "inbound" leads that contact you and have already taken themselves through your online educational sales process.

Is Thought Leadership the Kale of the Marketing World?

Everyone's talking about it. The web is full of discussions about it. Apparently, though, even though everyone says they're on board, not everyone's doing it after all. But if there are so many benefits to implementing a thought leadership strategy, why are so few small businesses doing it?

We believe it's because most of the writing, talk, and buzz around thought leadership is academic and theoretical, and many of the case studies highlighting the merits of thought leadership focus on prominent CEOs and large businesses, so most small business owners think it doesn't apply to them.

Most importantly, until right now there have been no practical, straightforward guides that explain how thought leadership applies to small businesses. Until now, finding a step-by-step process on how to DO thought leadership in real life was like finding a unicorn. But not anymore.

That's what we've done here. Put the powerful potential of thought leadership into the hands of people in small businesses. Busy people. People who know their stuff already but need an easy way to put that knowledge to work for them.

In this book, we will:

- Define what thought leadership is and how it applies to small businesses.
- Outline how thought leadership is one of the best ways to support your business growth over time.
- Explain where thought leadership fits in your marketing and business mix.
- Provide you with a practical guide to help you through the three-step process of "doing" thought leadership – so you will know exactly what you need to do, how you need to do it, and when.
- Share examples of real life companies that have unleashed their thought leadership power in their markets and gotten great results more easily than you might imagine.

Are you ready to dive in? When you turn the page, you're going to get a firm grasp on what thought leadership is, see what's possible for your business when you start doing thought leadership, find out where it fits into your current marketing mix, and discover why YOUR business type is the perfect match for the power of this strategy.

Becoming a thought leader has made it much easier to get new ideas out to the world, to know what new products to build, to find users to try out new technologies, and, of course, for HubSpot to get paying customers. Without the reach I had, I'm not sure HubSpot would be the company it is today, which includes having 900+ employees and being publicly traded on the NYSE (ticker: HUBS). HubSpot has gotten thousands of customers because of our thought leadership in the marketing space.

Dharmesh Shah, Founder of Hubspot

CHAPTER 2

WHAT IS THOUGHT LEADERSHIP ?

…Like nailing Jello to a tree.

Janeane Garofalo

D efining thought leadership can seem to be a bit like nailing Jello to a tree. You know, wiggly and jiggly – it doesn't hold still or remaining static, and it's downright difficult to nail down. But we are going to do our best to break it down for you in practical terms, so you will have a firm grip on what you can do to take action and become a thought leader in your industry.

What Is Thought Leadership?

We've seen thought leadership defined many ways. We touched on one definition in chapter one, but let's take a closer look at what the experts are saying to provide more clarity:

- Wikipedia's definition is "content that is recognized by others as innovative, covering

trends and topics that influence an industry."
(https://en.wikipedia.org/wiki/Thought_leader)

- An article in *Forbes* defined a thought leader as "a person or firm that is not only recognized but who also profits from the recognition of their authority."
  (http://www.forbes.com/sites/russprince/2012/03/16/what-is-a-thought-leader/)

- Daniel Rasmus of Fast Company shared this definition: "Thought leadership should be an entry point to a relationship. It should intrigue, challenge, and inspire even people already familiar with a company. It should help start a relationship where none exists, and it should enhance existing relationships."
  (http://www.fastcompany.com/3003897/golden-rules-creating-thoughtful-thought-leadership)

For the purpose of this book, we are defining thought leadership as:

"How brands can position themselves as leaders in their fields, industries, and sectors – not just by what they say, but by actually demonstrating their expertise, values, unique points of view, and the ability to answer their target audiences' biggest questions."

As you can see, the definitions of thought leadership vary slightly, but there are common threads – unique points of view and building relationships through education. While some people take an expansive view of the term and weave corporate culture and strategy into the definition, others focus more on content. All definitions, however, point to a thought leader being someone whose voice is an authentic and valuable addition to dialogue, rather than being a distraction or a mere attention-seeking ploy. When done right, thought leadership is as valuable to a business or brand as the product or service it sells.

The truth is, establishing yourself as a thought leader calls for consistent, pedal-to-the-metal effort. It should be a point of entry to your relationship with customers and prospects – starting new relationships and enhancing already-existing relationships. So it is an entirely new way of presenting yourself to others and relating to them. As a thought leader, you are becoming an authority on topics relevant to your target audience by answering their most pressing questions.

Keeping your customers and prospects in the forefront of everything you do is the key to thought leadership. You let THEM set your agenda. You let THEM ask the questions for which you will provide the answers. Your success as a thought leader is defined by how well you communicate your unique point of view, answer their questions, and meet their needs.

> *A few pieces of advice about becoming a thought leader: Don't focus on becoming a thought leader, focus on helping people. Build experiences, and share those experiences with others who would benefit from them. Stay open to input from your readership. Don't be overly self-indulgent. Your thought leadership should be about your followers and what they need, not about you. Put your ego aside and learn. No matter how good you are, there is always more to learn.*
>
> **Dharmesh Shah, Founder of Hubspot**

So How Does Thought Leadership Apply to Your Business in Real Life?

At a practical level, thought leadership is accomplished by continuously educating your audience and communicating your unique point of view through various forms of content, such as blog posts, articles, and case studies.

While many people in the marketing world refer to thought leadership as simple content marketing, this is not entirely true. It's not as much about the act of creating blog posts, articles, case studies, and whitepapers as it is about what you put into that content that makes you a thought leader.

The key here is that you're not just educating your audience on the features and benefits of your specific products or services, but on important topics and best practices in your industry overall. Moreover, you hold and communicate a unique point of view that sets you apart, a point of view that flows through all of your communications. You are identifying your target audience's biggest questions and using educational content to provide the answers. Through this content, you will build the sense of confidence your customers and prospects have in you, boost your brand recognition, and give your audience the information they are seeking. It's like content marketing 2.0.

Reaching your target audience in this way is much more powerful than using fancy – and pricey – brochures, slick ads, and email blasts. It also gives you the opportunity to set industry trends instead of just doing what the other guys are doing. You become the innovator – which automatically sets you apart from the rest.

Thought leadership isn't just for individuals. In fact, we are going to cover how your business can use thought leadership to shape people's perception of your company and its products – the right way.

The ultimate goal, of course, is to increase your profits. But as a thought leader you want to focus on garnering respect and recognition, so you can hold a place of authority in your prospects' eyes. While it's true that much of the work you do to engage in thought leadership is focused on developing relationships with your target audience, the objective is to position yourself so you are *SOUGHT OUT* for your expertise.

What Are the Benefits of Thought Leadership for a Business?

We believe thought leadership is one of the most overlooked marketing strategies for businesses – especially for small business owners who often believe thought leadership is only for very large organizations. This strategy has the best potential for success over the long term. It is a best-kept marketing secret, and we know everyone likes a good marketing secret – especially when it has been proven to be so effective.

Here are the top six reasons to adopt a thought leadership strategy for your business:

1. **You don't need a huge budget.**

   Many businesses operate on a lean budget – especially small businesses – and don't have extra money to spend on expensive marketing tactics and campaigns. And while implementing a successful thought leadership system will require your time and energy, it won't require a huge budget. Thought leadership is more about working smartly and efficiently so you earn your customers instead of buying them.

2. **You can differentiate yourself from the competition – including your larger competitors.** The reality is that not many small business owners are doing thought leadership at all, and many larger businesses are not doing it very well. This means if you install the right thought leadership system into your business, over time, your brand may appear more credible, trustworthy, and authoritative than companies twice your size.

Even better, thought leadership is a great way to position your company, products, and services as unique in the minds of your target audience, which makes you more interesting and memorable. People want to work with someone who is not a follower – they want to work with an innovator. As a thought leader, you become that innovator.

3. **You reduce the need to sell.**
   This is a big one. With the right thought leadership strategy in place, you set up a system where you educate and move your customers through your buying process online – so when they contact you, they are already sold and ready to buy, which significantly reduces the need for traditional sales.

4. **You will create awareness for your products and services.**

   The goal of most traditional marketing (like advertising) is to create awareness for your products and services. Thought leadership will do this, too, and in a way that is more effective because it's more educational and less salesy. And can't we all just agree that "salesy" is OUT? Consumers are tired of this old, worn-out marketing approach, which is why thought leadership breathes new life into your marketing efforts.

   Thought leadership gives you the opportunity to create a personality for your brand and business – you become memorable, unique, and interesting to your target audience. This is especially true for solopreneurs, entrepreneurs, and business owners who ARE their business.

   Once you are well known and trusted, you can easily create a word-of-mouth marketing machine, generating leads and referrals like never before. Being a thought leader gives you access to people and partners who can make things happen for you. It gives *you* the status and authority needed to move things in a new direction as well as the clout to implement real progress and widespread innovation.

People want to affiliate with those who are well known and in-the-know. Becoming a thought leader automatically gets you a ticket to the cool kids' table. You will be more likely to receive invitations to join corporate boards and participate in industry-wide committees, increasing your visibility and raising your profile locally and even nationally or (gulp!) internationally.

5. **Your initial investment will continue to work for you over time.**
   With a lot of traditional marketing, you launch a campaign, you execute, tally your results, and then it's over. Then you have to pay and launch again. One of the primary benefits of thought leadership is that it's an incremental strategy, where the educational content you share continues to work for you over time – unlike paid tactics that go away quickly.

For example, if you create one blog post that answers a key customer question, it becomes a page on your website. You may launch an initial campaign and share that page via social media, email, and even through paid advertising. But your campaign doesn't end there.

That one page, answering that one important customer question, starts to rank in Google. So when your target audience is searching for a solution to their problem, your blog post comes up. Not just today, but next month and next year. So imagine you create two blog posts a month. At the end of the year, you will have 24 web pages answering 24 important customer questions all ranking separately on Google and working for you.

And it doesn't end there. You can re-share and re-purpose all of these blog posts over time, which is just one example of how thought leadership as a marketing strategy is an investment, not a one-off tactic.

6. **You will improve your search engine rankings at a low cost.**

    Creating content as a thought leader costs very little but can increase your business's search engine ranking. That's just the truth. Google updates have rendered those old, recycled, keyword-laden articles useless. The Internet powerhouse is now recognizing valuable content from real people and placing it in the coveted top spots of search engine rankings. When you are creating thought leadership content, it is answering real questions that real people have, offering innovative solutions, and meeting your target audience's specific needs for information – and this is exactly what Google is all about in the post-Panda algorithm update era.

What does it cost you? If you write it yourself, nothing. If you hire a writer, something. But even if you must hire a professional writer, the investment is small compared to the price tag on most other paid advertising and marketing tasks. The return on investment is undeniable.

At a very practical level, thought leadership can:
- Increase traffic to your website.
- Enable more people to find your business.
- Achieve more sales from better customers in less time.
- Screen out the bad clients.
- Encourage returning customers.
- Put your business in the forefront of people's minds.
- Help you to stop competing on price alone. When customers buy into your unique approach to solving their problems, price isn't the primary selling point.
- Attract better talent – people who are drawn to your approach and leadership.

- Generate strong leads for your sales force, which will increase morale and decrease the time it takes to close leads.
- Lead to product innovation.
- Bring meaning to your work; when you claim a unique position as a thought leader, it helps you to understand and clarify why you are doing what you do.
- And yes – improve your SEO rankings, which will facilitate all of the above!

What Types of Businesses Need Thought Leadership?

Only all of them!

1. Large businesses, small business, and solopreneurs
2. Businesses that target other businesses or consumers
3. Businesses that sell products or provide services

Yes, you got it – nearly all businesses from every industry can benefit from true thought leadership. If you have competitors and are trying to earn the respect and loyalty of a target audience – which covers most people in business – thought leadership will set you apart.

The barriers to entry into thought leadership for your business are pretty low at the moment. Sure, lots of businesses and entrepreneurs are attempting what they identify as thought leadership, but when you break it down, what they are doing is little more than basic content creation that involves information about their products and services with a few thought leadership words thrown in for good measure. Very few businesses are doing thought leadership on a consistent and systematic basis – which is the only way to see results.

If your business can offer a depth of knowledge and deliver fresh insights to your target audience's problems and needs, you can easily transform your industry as a thought leader. Not too many are doing this right now, which means you will stand out in all the right ways.

How Does Thought Leadership Work as a Marketing Strategy?

One of the biggest challenges for business owners is figuring out where thought leadership fits into their overall business and marketing strategy or system.

What do we mean by strategy? It's really just identifying your ideal client and what makes your company different from the competition.

Before we tackle thought leadership, let's step back and consider whether you even need to have a defined marketing strategy and system in place FIRST. The simple answer is no.

The great news is that thought leadership will fit in well with your existing marketing strategy. If you don't yet have a marketing strategy in place – and don't worry, many business owners don't – this guide will help you define your strategy at the same time you implement your thought leadership system. Working smarter, not harder is the name of the thought leadership game!

It's trite I know, but just do something, do it. Get your Twitter account going. Get yourself out there and be authentic. I'm a big believer in this idea of authenticity. As my favorite consulting author Peter Block says, "Authenticity is the ability to just say what you see." Put into words what you personally are experiencing and don't be afraid of it.

Ed Kless, Radio Talk Show Host, Partner Department and Strategy for Sage Group

---

So Where Does Thought Leadership Fit into Your Marketing Mix?

Now that you understand what thought leadership is and the benefits it offers for your marketing, there's another important question to address: *Where does it fit into your marketing plan?* Forget the abstract ideas and philosophies. You need practical advice that will help you know what to do to take action.

Let's take a look at how marketing has changed in the last 10 years, and what you need to know about the new rules to succeed. Then, we'll dive into a discussion of some of the best practices for creating a solid marketing strategy and how you can incorporate thought leadership in light of the new rules and your marketing system.

The New Rules of Marketing

Before the Internet, marketing was different.

"Traditional marketing" was all about spending money to interrupt your audience with your sales message while they were doing something else – an ad while they were reading a magazine or watching TV, a telemarketing call, a knock on the door during dinner, or a piece of mail.

This was effective, especially for larger businesses with big budgets, because they had complete control over their message, where their message was placed, and who saw it. Better yet, the message traveled in one direction only – from the business to the consumer – so the big business had the last word.

With the Internet – and forums, chat boards, and social media – marketing changed in three key ways:

1. Companies and advertisers could no longer completely control their message, and the audience could question what they were saying and talk back.
2. Businesses could get many of their messages across for free – through their websites, social media, and other online forums.
3. Buyers didn't have to wait for businesses to advertise to know what's out there – they could search for products and services online. This leveled the playing field, as savvy business owners – including smaller businesses and solopreneurs – could now be found and appear just as large and credible as their larger competitors.

As a result of these changes:

- Today's buyers are much more savvy and don't respond the same way to marketing or sales messages. They don't immediately trust that what a company claims about their products or services is true just because they say it.
- Marketing is less about pitching and selling and more about educating and informing.

- Nearly every buyer searches for a business online before buying – so the ability to not only be found online but to provide buyers with the information they need is essential.

The Marketing Hourglass

The Marketing Hourglass (a trademarked concept from Duct Tape Marketing) is a simple and easy model to use in developing your marketing strategy and system. You can find a diagram of the Marketing Hourglass below and downloadable version at this link: https://ducttapemarketing.com/build-marketing-hourglass/

In a very simple but powerful way, the Marketing Hourglass mimics the steps *most* buyers go through when buying a product or service. If you use the Marketing Hourglass as a blueprint, simply make sure you fill in each buying stage and give your buyers clear steps to move through your process.

Here are the Marketing Hourglass Buying Stages:

Know
Before your audience can buy your product or service, they have to first KNOW that you exist.

Like

Once they know you exist, your audience needs to LIKE your company – your story and brand need to resonate with them.

Trust

Liking your company is not enough. Your audience needs to TRUST that your products and services will do what you claim, and that your business will be around for the long term.

Try

Once your audience trusts you, they need a low-risk way to TRY your products or services for free or at a low cost.

Buy

Now that your audience is ready to BUY, you need to have a process or system in place to make this as easy as possible, and to wow them – because this stage is the best time to create referrals.

Repeat

Your existing customers are one of your best sources for continual business. You need to make sure you keep them happy so they will REPEAT buy from you, and consider ways to cross-sell.

Refer

Staying on your customers' minds and continually educating and providing value to them is one of the best ways to get them to REFER you to other businesses. And referrals create immediate TRUST and shorten the sales cycle for new customers.

The Marketing Hourglass can be used by companies of any size. This means you can start small by just adding one or two items to each stage of your Marketing Hourglass, and then add as many items as you need to grow your business.

Below is an example of a really simple Marketing Hourglass with just one or two items in each category:

Know	Like	Trust	Try	Buy	Repeat	Refer
Google Adwords and/or Facebook Ads	*Weekly blog posts.* *The 'About' page on your website*	*A case study from a happy client*	*An eBook outlining your unique program*	*A new client welcome kit with a surprise bonus*	*A monthly newsletter*	*A letter of introduction to you from a strategic partner*

In Chapter 7, we'll show you how you can turn your Marketing Hourglass strategy into a marketing system in real life.

Where Does Thought Leadership Fit In?

You may have heard the terms 'Inbound Marketing' and 'Content Marketing.' Essentially, these are two complementary strategies that harness the power of the new rules of marketing – they also fit nicely into the Marketing Hourglass strategy.

Inbound marketing is all about using educational content (the content marketing part) to enable your audience to find your business online. Once they've found you, you strategically use that content to move them through your buying process (i.e. the Marketing Hourglass) and give them ways to contact you when they are ready to buy.

For example, we helped one of our clients, a leadership coach, write an eBook outlining their overall system, along with a series of blog posts. We created a website landing page for the eBook, which required prospects to provide their email address in exchange for downloading the book. Each week, we would post one of the blog articles on the website and share the link to the blog post over social media. The call-to-action on each blog post was to download the eBook. Because we now had their email addresses, we were able to continue the marketing process.

Thought leadership forms your overall content strategy, where you define your audience, identify their key problems, hone your unique and authentic voice, and determine your unique point of view. This strategy inspires the type of content you create.

Inbound marketing is the structure and system you set up to share your content based on the Marketing Hourglass stages. The content you create is what you share in your inbound marketing system.

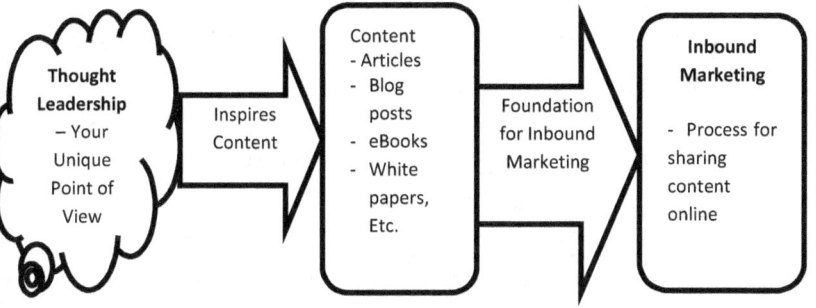

Can you create a marketing strategy and inbound marketing system without thought leadership?

You absolutely can, but it will not be nearly as effective.

Why? Because with a generic content/inbound marketing system, you can share content and put steps in place to move your audience through your buying system. However, that will lack a consistent voice and point of view, you won't have a strong handle on your target audience and their main problems, and your content will be more ad-hoc and inconsistent.

Thought leadership is the engine behind content/inbound marketing. By taking the time to define your thought leadership strategy up front, you will be clear on your audience and their problems, as well as your authentic voice, unique point of view, and core difference. This will come across clearly and consistently in all of the content you create and share, making you more interesting, memorable, and yielding much more powerful results. If you have a clear strategy and voice, your audience will ultimately see you as more trustworthy and authoritative.

Coming up, we will give you a simple three-step process to "do" thought leadership.

Becoming a thought leader wasn't intentional. I just started writing. People started following my blog. The reach grew, and I guess somewhere along the way, I crossed that magical line into thought leadership. What I did is simple: Have some novel thoughts and then write about them and talk about them to see if others agree or disagree. Spark conversations. Help people apply the ideas. Recruit others to help spread the word.

Dharmesh Shah, Founder of Hubspot

CHAPTER 3

THOUGHT LEADERSHIP FOR SOLOPRENEURS AND SMALL BUSINESS OWNERS

Put another log on the fire.
Cook me up some bacon and some beans.
And go out to the car and change the tire.
Wash my socks and sew my old blue jeans.
Come on, baby, you can fill my pipe,
And then go fetch my slippers.
And boil me up another pot of tea.
Then put another log on the fire, babe,
And come and tell me why you're leaving me.

"Put Another Log on the Fire"
The Outlaws

Sound a bit like your life as a solopreneur or small business owner? The joke is that as a business owner, you get to work half days – whichever 12 hours you'd like!

Have you heard of Google's famed "20 Percent Time" policy? That's where employees are allowed – scratch that, **expected** – to spend a full 20 percent of their work time working on independent research projects. It's like being sent off to the corner of a library to think great thoughts and report back.

As a small business owner or solopreneur, the thought of being free to think deep thoughts about your field for 20 percent of your work time – or even to have five minutes to think about much at all – probably seems laughable. You don't get paid to sit and think – you have to do it on the fly, in the trenches, and often on the back burner.

The elephant in the room just trumpeted. How are you supposed to be a thought leader if you're already kicking and paddling as fast as you can just to keep your head above the rising tide of your to-do list?

That same elephant has an ugly cousin – one that points out the fact that doing all the research, writing, and publishing typically considered part and parcel of becoming a thought leader can just be plain old hard. It's even harder when you add in an implied requirement that your topic has to be completely original. After all, if you're writing the same story everyone in your field has already told, you're not a leader. Right?

No wonder most attempts at thought leadership by small business owners and solopreneurs usually end up looking suspiciously like repackaged versions of what you might find in fifty other blogs in your industry. The drive for thought leadership has resulted in a population boom among parrots.

So, give up. Right?

Of course not.

Sure, you're small. Sure, you're probably underfunded to some extent. Sure, you're already working your tail off and don't have even a minute to spare in the quest to think great thoughts.

Lay all of that aside, and focus on what you already know. It might stretch your self-perception to crown yourself an expert, but if you've been at it (whatever your 'it' might be) for a while, you're very likely an expert. You know much more than your average customer – that's why your customers come to you for the products and services you sell. Especially for your services. If they knew what you know, or could do what you do as well as you do or as quickly and effectively as you do it, you'd be out of business.

It's like the story of the plumber who was called out to a customer's home to fix a leaky pipe. The plumber took all of about three minutes to fix the leak, then handed the customer a bill for $228. The customer was shocked, complaining that the plumber had only spent a few minutes fixing the problem. The plumber replied that while the replacement part only cost $28, knowing where and how to fix the leak had taken him decades of practice – and that was worth the additional $200.

You Know Your Stuff. They Don't.

You know a whole lot about your field, but your prospects and customers may not. They've got questions – lots of questions. Maybe they don't even know enough to ask the questions they should be asking. For sure, they don't know who's trustworthy enough to guide them to the solution they truly need.

That's where you come in. You can be the hero and save the day. You might not be THE thought leader in your field, but you can be THEIR thought leader, and that's what really matters.

Even though you might not be on the cusp of some award-winning discovery in your industry, you're pretty smart. You're always learning more about your field. You follow the trends and developments that allow you to stay current. You probably even go to trade shows, invest in continuing education, read publications in your field, and network with colleagues who do what you do, too. That's a lot of learning you're already doing – and you've probably given some thought to all you've learned, even informally.

How much of that learning do you think your customers and prospects have done? Think they could sort through the pile of baloney, myths, and shysters in your industry to suss out the truth? Not a chance.

What if you could wade through all of the junk circulating online (and offline) about your industry and give your prospects and customers the scoop on what's true, valuable, and actionable? That might be your entrance into the realm of thought leadership on a local level.

We Said the *L*- Word

The word *local* brings up another point we need to ponder here. If you're a small business owner or solopreneur serving customers mainly in your local area, you're not really in competition with super-sized corporations that serve a global customer base. It might look like these titans of trade can whop you any day of the week (and maybe they can, in some ways) – but by now you've probably realized that a growing percentage of people prefer to do business with local companies. They know they're more likely to receive outstanding customer service with a small, local business versus being customer #928851032245 with a multi-national corporation.

So, what if you focused your thought leadership efforts in your local area? What if you aimed at being THE go-to (whatever you are) for your city or town? Perhaps your products and services perform differently in your area compared to how they'd perform elsewhere. Maybe your local customer and prospect base face challenges that are specific to your area.

For example, let's say you're an electrician. Let's say you've noticed that you get an inordinate number of service calls from homeowners in one particular swanky neighborhood. The homes are older, the neighborhood gentrified. The folks who are moving in are hip and trendy. They'd like to be do-it-yourselfers, but they don't have the skills. You can imagine their homes being featured on one of those home improvement shows.

You've learned the ins and outs of these older homes because you've been working in that neighborhood for decades. While other electricians might be able to poke around and get the job done, you know exactly how those homes were wired decades ago. It's almost like you can see through the walls!

Think a homeowner in that neighborhood might be very interested to hear your thoughts on pretty much anything related to the wiring of these homes? You could talk about wiring quirks that might pose a safety risk. You could discuss modern gadgetry that works – or doesn't work – in those homes. You might even be able to provide wiring workarounds that will actually work, whereas your "big guy" competitor would be stuck trying to figure out how to make a one-size-fits-all solution fit.

Small? You're Not Off the Hook

You're busy. You're probably never going to be paid to think deep thoughts. You're going to face some challenges as you implement your thought leadership strategy (but you're not alone in that). You, however, are also holding a step-by-step guide created by people just like you – small business owners and solopreneurs.

Pow! Right in the excuse-maker.

To butcher the quote from the famous motivational speaker, Stuart Smalley:

> *"You're good enough.*
> *You're smart enough.*
> *Your business is big enough.*
> *And doggone it, people like you."*

Ready to take the first step in developing your thought leadership plan? There are only three simple steps in the whole process, so once you tackle the first, you're a third of the way there. Let's do this!

CHAPTER 4

THREE STEPS TO "DOING" THOUGHT LEADERSHIP

So now that you know what thought leadership is, and why it's an important strategy for solopreneurs and small business owners, are you ready to learn how to actually "do" all this thought leadership stuff?

Well, we're ready to show you. In the next three chapters, we'll outline a step-by-step process to implement thought leadership into your business:

- Step 1: Develop a Thought Leadership Mindset

- Step 2: Build Your Thought Leadership Foundation

- Step 3: Activate Your Thought Leadership System

Before You Get Started – Download Your "Do Leadership Plan Template":

To make this process as simple and practical as possible, we've created a Do Leadership Plan Template that you can download.

You can refer to this template as you work through the next three chapters, creating your Do Leadership Plan as you go. We've also included two sample plans for reference. One plan is for a mid-size technology company that sells to other businesses and the other is for a solopreneur. Use these sample plans to give you ideas as you build your own Do Leadership Plan.

DOWNLOAD NOW HERE:
http://ducttapepublishing.com/wp-content/uploads/2016/06/Do-Leadership-Plan-Template.pdf

CHAPTER 5

STEP ONE:
DEVELOP A THOUGHT LEADERSHIP MINDSET

Think like a man of action, act like a man of thought.

Henri Bergson

Effective thought leadership is the masterful mix of right thinking, right action, and right motivation. Stop at just thinking great (but obscure and unpublished) thoughts, and at best you'll be a brilliant philosopher in your niche. Act without strategy and forethought, and you'll find yourself running with and around the pack – but not leading it. Think and act with the wrong motivation, and it'll all be for nothing.

The first step of our three-step process for masterful DO leadership is all in your head. Getting the enticing business results promised by the concept of thought leadership requires developing the right mindset first.

In this chapter, we will:

- Outline the five key elements of a thought leadership mindset
- Discuss whether or not you can outsource thought leadership
- Explore who in your organization would make the best thought leader

The Five Key Elements of a Thought Leadership Mindset

In this section, we're going to help prepare you mentally by discussing the five key elements of a thought leadership mindset.

#1: Use Your Authentic Voice

Oscar Wilde nailed it: "Be yourself; everyone else is already taken."

A thought leader, by definition, has to be genuine, transparent, and authentic. Mimic another thought leader in your industry and your message is automatically downgraded to "me too" status. Craft a thought leader persona that bears no resemblance to reality, and you'll live in constant (and justified) fear of being revealed as a fraud.

You don't have to portray yourself as an all-knowing savant. It's okay to cop to not knowing everything. In fact, being transparent doesn't just add to your likeability – it speaks to your credibility. And the more credible you appear, the more your audience will begin to trust you as their guide and as an authority in the industry.

The first person you must convince about your unique expertise is yourself. You don't need to believe that you are the world's foremost expert on your industry, but you do need to grasp the reality that you know a whole lot more about your industry than the average person.

Because you've been at it for some time, you know enough about your specialty to serve as sort of a niche-specific superhero for everyday people. You're uniquely equipped to be the tour guide for the uninitiated in your market.

You've given enough off-hours thought to the intricacies of your field that you can provide valuable advice to buyers who need to make important decisions – and you can serve as the voice of experience, guiding them to make those decisions wisely.

#2: Harness the Power of Story

You only need to research thought leadership theory for about 47 seconds before you find references to the power of storytelling. Two examples show up in most accounts of the rise of storytelling:

- John Deere's *The Furrow* publication, which educated farmers about how new agricultural technology could make them more successful in the business of farming.

- The World's Largest Store (WLS) radio show in the 1920's, sponsored by Sears-Roebuck, marked the company's bid to find its way into households all over the nation. Sears sold the radios, owned the radio station, and created the programming that was second only to The Grand Old Opry in its day.

Storytelling is at the heart of effective content marketing – and there's a good reason for it. If you think way back to when you were a little kid, probably the most magical words you ever heard a teacher or librarian utter were, "It's story time, children!" Those words were often followed by, "Once upon a time…" – words that instantly transported you into a realm ruled by your imagination.

Stories touch emotions, and emotions drive sales. Stories connect with your buyer's emotions in a way that no other messaging style can match.

Neuroscience and behavioral sciences back this up. In a nutshell, they say that it's our unconscious mind that drives us (including our buying behavior). Traditional marketing targets the conscious mind, following a predictable formula: headline, benefits, risk removal, call-to-action. Storytelling targets the unconscious mind – both the Mammalian brain (emotions, memories, hormones, and moods) and the Reptilian brain (fight or flight, survival functions, and automatic responses).

Erik du Plessis, in *The Advertised Mind*, says that the Reptilian brain rules rapid decision-making, overruling logic and conscious thought and driving buying decisions. Storytelling touches that process, setting off mental alarms that speak to the pain of missing out. The Reptilian brain makes the buying decision, the Mammalian brain approves it, and the conscious mind justifies it.

The nature of content marketing is crafting and telling your story – and integrating storytelling throughout all of your communications with your customers and prospects.

Here are just a few benefits you get from storytelling:

- **Stories humanize your brand.**
  People relate best to people, not abstract ideas and brands. When you make it personal, sharing your company's story, or, even better, the stories of those you serve, your audience is inspired. "Selling" messages pales in comparison to sharing perspectives that build a human connection.

- **Stories make complex ideas simple.**
  Your message can leave your audience lost if it's difficult to understand. Stories enable you to "show" rather than to explain. They paint a picture of what you mean, how your idea plays out in reality, and how the concept impacts real humans. When your audience gets what's at stake, they take action.

- **Stories make you memorable.**
  Think of story-driven TV commercials that stick with you, even years later – including the brand and the product. Remember the Folgers Coffee commercials featuring a son returning from college? Or, the Mean Joe Green Coca-Cola ad (Hey kid, catch!)? Stories are memorable and shareable.

- **Stories establish your authority.**
  Shoppers are skeptical. These questions about your products and services rattle around in their minds until you answer them: Will it really work? Will it deliver the benefits they promise? When you share stories about real-life successes, you provide information about your business – but even more powerfully, you offer proof that yours is the solution these shoppers have been searching for.

#3: Build Credibility and Trust

Before Spiderman's uncle quipped it, good old Anonymous once said, "With great power comes great responsibility." There is an inherent power you get, and a corresponding responsibility you must accept, when you become a thought leader.

While there's no oath you must swear as you take this position, human decency (ultimately enforced by the marketplace) demands that you act in such a way that you're doing good where you can and avoiding causing harm. Understanding human nature and crafting your thought leadership strategy to sync with it is good. Exploiting it to manipulate people into doing business with you is not only bad, it's short-sighted and a sure way to earn the kind of exposure nobody wants.

A thought leader is first a leader (hey, it's in the name!), and good leaders aim to protect and serve those who follow them. Your motives in establishing your role as a thought leader in your marketplace will become evident to your audience. Best to aim at giving value first. The law of reciprocity will take effect naturally, and you'll be rewarded in due time – but only in proportion to the value you give.

#4: Educational Focus

Sy Syms said it best: "An educated consumer is our best customer."

Where traditional marketing is primarily aimed at persuading prospects to part with their money, thought leadership has a different thrust. In it for the long haul, your goal is to educate your audience rather than just to sell them.

In the long run, an educated consumer truly is a superior customer. Not only can educated consumers recognize quality when they see it, they're also likely to become better brand ambassadors who can extol your company's virtues effectively.

It's been said that while people love to buy stuff, they hate being sold. As you produce thought leadership content that educates your audience, you'll provide them with all the information they need to evaluate their situation, your products and services, and how well they mesh. They sell themselves, convincing themselves that doing business with you is the best possible option.

#5 Hold a Unique Point of View

It's not enough to be authentic and tell your story. You also need to hold a unique point of view that your audience can recognize and is woven throughout everything you say.

But what is your unique point of view? Ask 10 small business owners and nine will tell you they don't have one. The reality is that every small business owner holds a unique point of view – the trouble is that it isn't always easy to see your own greatness.

So if you're one of those business owners who isn't clear on your core difference and unique point of view, here are some questions that can help, along with some places you might look at your existing content to gain more insight.

How are You Different?

Before considering your unique point of view, step back and think for a minute about your core difference. Once you have a better understanding of what makes you and your company different, it's much easier to move on to determine your unique point of view.

What Makes You Different in Each of the Following Areas?

- Your system or process
- Your personality
- Your services, packages, processes, or courses
- Your background or expertise
- Your style or creativity

- When or how you offer something
- Your price or pricing method
- Something else?

Questions to Hone In on Your Core Difference and Unique Point of View

Take a minute to consider your answers to the following questions. They will provide clues on your unique point of view. Once you've answered the questions that seem most relevant to you and your business, which questions and answers stand out more than the others?

- What do you consider yourself an expert in?
- In what areas do others recognize you as an expert?
- What have others recognized you as an expert in?
- What customer problems do you understand more than anyone else?
- What are the three core things you would tell others about your business?
- If you knew a close friend was going to buy a competitive product or service, what advice would you give them?
- What about your industry bothers you?
- What are some key misconceptions about your industry that you want others to know?
- What messages do other companies put out that bother you?
- What do other companies in your industry do that you feel misleads customers?

Ideas & Sources of Insight

If you're still having trouble nailing down your core difference and unique point of view, here are some sources you can turn to for more ideas and insight:

- Customer surveys
- Customer comment cards and feedback forms
- Non-customer surveys (e.g. LinkedIn Q&A or contest surveys)
- Inbound call center/help desk
- Questions from sales meetings
- Questions from consulting engagements or service calls
- Vendor announcements
- Vendor offers
- Governmental or regulatory rule changes
- Industry expert comments
- Competitor actions or announcements
- Alliance partner feedback, issues, or initiatives
- Social media posts by industry experts, competitors, or target market suspects

Can You Outsource Thought Leadership?

Well, there's one tiny bit of bad news – the quick answer is maybe.

Because thought leadership requires authenticity, a unique point of view and voice that rings true, and a story that is trusted and credible, you can never completely outsource your thought leadership program. While you can hire someone to help you with the implementation, your audience will smell something fishy if you outsource your thought leadership entirely.

Raise their hackles, and every story you tell, and every example you give will build your audience's skepticism rather than their assurance that they can trust you. Plus, imagine the awkwardness and disingenuousness of a moment when you're called upon to tell a story that's not even yours – those are not shoes you want to step into.

It's kind of like hiring a personal trainer or a coach. You can't pay him or her to diet and exercise for you. Similarly, you can't outsource your 'thinking.' There is no Cyrano de Bergerac solution for thought leadership – you simply must tell your unique story. The good news is that you can get help.

You Don't Have to Go it Alone

Just because you can't outsource your thought leadership entirely doesn't mean you're on your own. You can get help, especially when it comes to developing your thought leadership strategy, learning thought leadership best practices, creating your thought leadership system, and getting your thought leadership content out into the world.

So while you – or someone in your organization – needs to be the thought leader, a writer, marketing consultant, or coach can partner with you to help you recognize and then convey your message through a collaborative process. You communicate your unique message, and they make it consumable.

Who in Your Organization Should Do Thought Leadership?

At this stage, if your company is bigger than just you, it's also important to determine who in your organization will be "doing" thought leadership. It may be one person, or it may be a few people – but for sure there's one group of people who simply cannot be the face of your thought leadership: your marketing department.

Why not the marketing team? While marketing plays an important role in establishing your thought leadership strategy, setting up your system, and helping you execute many of your thought leadership tactics, marketing cannot be the face of thought leadership for your organization.

Thought leadership starts at the top. The best candidates are people whose thoughts change the way we make decisions and take action. They generate new ideas, new options, and new perspectives on a consistent basis. They're the kind of people we watch for signals, reactions, and innovations. Thought leaders do not just execute ideas – they originate ideas and always have something new to share. Potential thought leaders to consider within in your organization could be employees who are subject matter experts and are respected in your field.

Often the thought leader for a business will be the founder, owner, or CEO. However, there are some instances where another subject matter expert in the company may make a better thought leader. For example, one medical device company we work with has a highly knowledgeable and well-spoken CEO. They also have, however, a Medical Director who is highly respected by the company's target audience. In this case, the Medical Director became the company's main thought leader.

Think about the different roles in your company and consider:

- Who is a subject matter expert?
- Which subject matter expert is most respected by your target audience?
- Which subject matter expert is both willing and able to be a thought leader for your company?
- Which subject matter expert is most likely to be with your company over the long term?

Back to our example with the medical device company: not only was their Medical Director highly respected in his field, he was also a member of the company's board of directors, so he was very likely to be bought in and remain a part of the company for many years.

If you choose someone other than yourself, the CEO, or business owner to be your main thought leader, it's imperative that you position yourself as a champion of your thought leadership program, and make sure that your thought leader is completely engaged and bought in. Without buy-in and support directly from the top, your thought leadership program will fizzle out.

Now, if you're a solopreneur or small business owner, it's a whole different story. You're it. The thought leader will be you.

Now that you've explored the five key elements of a thought leadership mindset, understand where you can and cannot outsource thought leadership, and have identified who in your organization will make the best thought leader, you're ready to move on to Step Two - building your thought leadership foundation. That's next!

CHAPTER 6

STEP TWO:
BUILD A THOUGHT LEADERSHIP FOUNDATION

*It is not the beauty of a building you should look at;
it's the construction of the foundation that will stand the test
of time.*

David Allan Coe

Step Two in the thought leadership development process is where you'll flex your strategy muscles. Before you can launch any of your thought leadership tactics, you need to build a strong thought leadership foundation. It's not some mysterious concoction – it's just a matter of knowing what you need, gathering it, and using it. Good news!

You only need four ingredients to get started on this second step and get you closer to reaping the benefits of a powerful thought leader position in your industry.

Here they are:

1. Strategy
2. Listening
3. Content
4. Online Assets

Your Thought Leadership Strategy

Certainly you didn't think you'd get through a book written by Duct Tape Marketers without a discussion on strategy, did you? Tsk, tsk.

There's a reason we don't do anything until the strategy is nailed down. Partially, it's because we're not big fans of wasting time and money. Partially, it's because we've seen how effective it is to develop a strategy with our clients first. You see, going through the strategy development process allows for a more surgically precise deployment of marketing tactics. You'll hit what you aim for!

Skip the strategy process, and your marketing efforts will be more like throwing a bunch of spaghetti at the wall, hoping something sticks. Huge corporations might be able to cover the costs of that kind of marketing disarray for a while, but if you need to run more budget-sensitive marketing efforts, you want to be able to zero in on your strategy before shooting the whole wad willy-nilly.

OK, off the soapbox for now. Let's look at the elements needed in a thorough strategy as you launch your thought leadership bid.

Your thought leadership strategy outlines:

- **Your Goals**
  Why are you doing thought leadership in the first place, and what are you hoping to achieve?

- **Your Internal Thought Leader Champion and Support System**
  Who in your organization is going to be your audience-facing thought leader, and who will support the thought leader in setting up the strategy and system and executing the tactics?

- **Your Audience**
  Who are you targeting with your thought leadership?

- **Your Business**
  Who in your business will participate in thought leadership? Who will be your main voice – or voices – and for what key areas?

- **Themes**
  What will your thought leadership themes be for the year? You'll need to plan monthly and

quarterly. This structure will make the creation of your thought leadership pieces much easier than it would be if you didn't have a framework to use.

- **Editorial Calendar**

  What events or important dates and specific topics will you focus on throughout the year to support your themes? Planning ahead will short-circuit needless panic, rushing, and missed opportunities. By planning a full editorial calendar, you'll have all your bases covered – and if an unforeseen opportunity arises, of course, there's nothing to keep you from jumping on it.

- **Marketing Mix**

  How does your thought leadership strategy fit into your overall marketing mix?

Listening

It might seem like thought leadership is all about saying what your prospects and customers need to hear – but the truth is, that's getting it all backwards. Before you utter a word, you must listen. Listen to your customers, listen to your stakeholders, listen to the people in your industry.

By setting up a listening station, you can stay on top of the latest information and industry trends. Best of all, your listening station can become an easy source of content ideas.

Begin by creating a list of all the companies, individuals, and organizations that are related to your business. This could include:

- Your audience (customers and prospects)
- Your competitors
- Your strategic partners
- Industry thought leaders
- Industry associations and events
- Industry publications

Messaging and Content

Now that you've created your thought leadership strategy and set up your listening station, it's time to consider your core messaging and content.

Messaging

When you get crystal clear about your messaging, making decisions about your content becomes a lot easier. Your thought leadership efforts will also take on a consistency that adds to your overall credibility. Just like you might create a house style for marketing materials, it's going to be helpful to create a centralized messaging guide.

You should cover the following angles:

- **Your point of view** – on the world, on your industry, on your customers
- **Your core message** – your customers' burning problem that you solve
- **Your methodology** – how you solve that problem

Here's an example from Duct Tape Marketing™:

- **Point of View:** Small businesses need a practical marketing system.
- **Core Message:** Simple, effective, affordable marketing.
- **Methodology:** Put strategy before tactics, use the Marketing Hourglass, publish educational content, create a total web presence, operate a lead generation trio, making a selling system, live by the marketing calendar.

If you engage with Duct Tape Marketing, there is a very specific reason you choose to do so. You know what the company stands for, what you will get, and how your purchase helps to achieve a goal you most likely have in common with that company. Their messaging is so clear that even a company outsider could easily determine whether any particular piece of marketing collateral aligns with the company's intentions.

Your company's messaging can be this clear as well, and you'll find that with extreme clarity comes a level of simplicity that makes content creation and marketing much simpler. You'll be less likely to wander off track or invest effort and resources into messaging that is off brand.

Content

For thought leadership, you have two main types of content – core (or foundational) content, and a selection of online assets. Your messaging should run straight through both with such all-out consistency that someone consuming your content – even without knowing it's yours – could reasonably guess where it came from. Let's take a look at both of these content types. Some businesses do one and ignore the other, but you'll know better in just a bit.

Core or Foundational Content

These are your main content pieces and will likely reside on your website for your audience to view or download on an ongoing basis. For some of these pieces, you may include an email gate, so your audience will have to enter a valid email address before downloading or accessing your content. Your core content will stay around for a while, and may even take on new forms as it's sliced, diced, and repurposed.

Your core content could include:

- Point of view eBook/video
- Speaker kit
- Main speaking presentation
- Media kit and bio
- Welcome video
- Book
- Online assets

Before you can launch your thought leadership tactics, you need to have permanent locations on the Internet to store your main content, launch your campaigns, and drive your audience back to in order to deposit them into the mouth of your sales funnel.

Your online assets could include:

- Website
- Blog
- Email system
- Social media pages

Thought Leadership Toolkit
Just like a household toolkit makes home improvement and repairs far more manageable than if you had to gather every nail, screw, washer, and hammer every single time you needed to tackle a project, you'll find your thought leadership toolkit helps make this project manageable as well. While the complexity of your

toolkit depends on the size and complexity of your business, the principle is the same no matter what form it takes – gather what you need for your thought leadership work so that it's handy when you need it.

Your toolkit might look a lot like a dashboard – even a simple spreadsheet with multiple tabs will work. You'll want to store and update the following information (HINT: You'll have all of this as you work through this book):

Strategy – Keep succinct, accurate reminders of each of the following:

- Your goals
- Your audience
- Your themes for the year

Listening Sources – Link to places where you can listen to the following:
- Your audience
- Your competitors
- Your strategic partners
- Industry thought leaders
- Industry associations
- Industry publications

Messaging Center – Keep this information handy:

- Your point of view
- Your one word
- Your core message

- Your methodology
- Your foundational topic

Core Content Asset Inventory – Provide easy access to the following:

- Point of view eBook/video
- Speaker kit
- Main speaking presentation
- Media kit and bio
- Welcome video
- Book
- What else do you have?

Editorial Calendar – Plan the content you'll publish this year, including:

- Speaking engagements
- Live events
- Case studies
- Social media
- Blogging
- Newsletters
- Special reports
- White papers
- Books
- Articles
- Magazines/eZines

Remember, you don't have to do it all at once! In fact, you shouldn't even try to, because that's the surest way to guarantee you'll get overwhelmed and flit to the next tactic instead of sticking, slow and steady, to one that's guaranteed to work long-term. Take this second step of the process at your own pace – that way you won't get stuck or stymied.

In every business task, there's a hard way and an easy way – a way you can go where it feels like you're winging it every step of the way, and a way that's proven to work. The essence of the thought leadership you're learning to broadcast is unique to you; the third step of the process isn't. If you'd like to cut your learning curve by learning the proven system of best practices we recommend, all you have to do is keep reading.

Becoming a thought leader certainly gotten me many more speaking engagements and consulting engagements. I think the other thing that it's done is it's really allowed me to carve out a unique position. I honestly cannot think of anybody that has a role similar to mine in such a large organization such as Sage anywhere.

Ed Kless, Radio Talk Show Host, Partner Department and Strategy for Sage Group

---

CHAPTER 7

STEP THREE:
ACTIVATE YOUR THOUGHT
LEADERSHIP SYSTEM

Everything must be made as simple as possible.
But not simpler.

Albert Einstein

Simplicity is at the core of this third step in the thought leadership marketing process – and the best systems are built upon simplicity. When you are building a system, the objective is to make tasks as streamlined and simple as possible, so you can repeat them again and again. You won't have to reinvent the wheel – it will all be laid out for you and any of your employees. You create a step-by-step process for accomplishing a task, and then you document that process and follow it, tweaking when necessary. You're far more likely to get uniformly excellent results by following a system rather than winging it every time. This is what it means to work smarter, not harder.

In this case, we are looking at creating a set of processes and action steps that bring your thought leadership strategy into the real world. With a system, everyone involved knows what to do, when to do it, and how to do it. Your system should include a checklist that will help ensure consistency no matter who is completing a task. Consistency is crucial if you want to be able to measure your effectiveness. Having your system documented also pays off when it comes time to train another team member. That's part of the beauty of a system – someone else can pick up the documentation, follow the steps, and get great results right from the start.

If you're feeling overwhelmed by the idea of creating and documenting processes for your thought leadership system, stop! Ultimately, it would be great to have every process documented. To start, though, it's important to be practical and realistic, which means starting smaller. Even if you only begin by adding one or two tactics to your system, that's enough to start seeing results.

Part of this process will be digging deep to get to know your audience, your niche, and even your top competitors. It takes some work, but you are building a solid foundation for your thought leadership system – a system that will be streamlined and duplicable. It will be well worth the effort.

See? *Simple.* Here are the basic elements that will comprise your Thought Leadership System. Answer these questions and you'll have a good start:

- Which tactics will you use?
- How will you distribute your thought leadership messages?
- Who will do the work?
- When are your thought leadership tasks scheduled to take place?

Thought Leadership Tactics

There are numerous tactics you can use to reach your audience with your thought leadership message. But which vehicle is right for your business? Or are all of them right?

Here is a list of some common thought leadership tactics you should consider. Remember, you don't have to do ALL of them. Just choose the ones that are right for your business right now. It's perfectly fine to start small. The idea here is just to get started. Remember, it's called DO Leadership!

Tactics that involve writing could include:

- Blog posts

- Articles in industry or consumer publications

- News releases

- Case studies

- eBooks

- White papers

- Research papers

- Position papers

- Surveys (summary of results)

- Books

Tactics that involve speaking could include:

- Presentations or keynote speaking at industry association meetings or events

- Participating in panel discussions at conferences

- Hosting workshops or seminars at industry events

- Hosting your own workshops or seminars

- Creating videos

- Holding podcasts

- Hosting webinars

Now that you've chosen some tactics to use, the next step is to consider how you'll distribute those tactics to your audience.

Some ways of distributing your content could include:

- Social media posts on Twitter, Facebook, LinkedIn, Google Plus, or other social media platforms

- Publishing articles on LinkedIn

- Publishing videos on YouTube or Vimeo

- Publishing presentations on SlideShare

- Sending out material via email or newsletter

- Posting to your website

- Sharing content with strategic partners and having them distribute it

- Advertising in print or online (Google AdWords, social media advertising, etc.)

Once again, you do not have to do ALL of these. The important thing is to make sure your thought leadership system is DO-able.

Now that you have an idea of the types of thought leadership tactics you can choose from, and some methods of delivering those tactics, we thought it would be a good idea to show you how you could turn these tactics and delivery methods into a system for a real live business.

Remember the Marketing Hourglass concept we introduced in Chapter 2? This is one of the best ways to organize your Thought Leadership Tactics into an overall strategy.

Organizing Your Content and Tactics into Your Marketing Strategy and System

As a brief reminder, the Marketing Hourglass outlines the buying stages most customers go through, along with the questions each stage answers:

- Know – how do prospects find and get to know your business?

- Like – how do you get prospects to like your business?

- Trust – how do you get prospects to trust your business?

- Try – how can prospects try your products or services in a low cost or risk-free way?

- Buy – how do you make the buying process as easy as possible for your customers – and wow them in the process?

- Repeat – how else will customers do business with you?

- Refer – how will your customers become your biggest advocates?

The Marketing Hourglass also serves as a super simple way to organize your content and tactics. And remember, you just have to choose at least one piece of content or tactic for each stage in the Marketing Hourglass, as in the example below:

Know	Like	Trust	Try	Buy	Repeat	Refer
Google Adwords and/or Facebook Ads.	Weekly blog posts. The About page on your website.	A case study from a happy client.	An eBook on outlining your unique program.	A new client welcome kit with a surprise bonus.	A monthly newsletter.	A letter of introduction to you from a strategic partner

Once you've chosen your types of content and tactics, it's time to consider how you will put this all together into what we call a Thought Leadership System.

Here's how the Marketing Hourglass example above might operate as a real life system:

1. Set up a landing page on your website where prospects can enter their name and email address to download the free eBook outlining your unique system (TRY).

2. Add a case study to your website (TRUST) and write an about page (LIKE) that tells your story.

3. Set up Google AdWords and Facebook Ads (KNOW) that directs prospects to the landing page for the free eBook.

4. Create a monthly newsletter (REPEAT) to send to every person on your email list (which will be continually populated with new email addresses from your free eBook download). The newsletter can include links to blog articles, customer success stories, and offers on new or additional products and services.

5. Create a new client welcome kit (BUY) outlining your onboarding process (and include a free gift

the customer didn't expect). Send this welcome kit to every new customer who buys from you.

6. Create a reverse introduction letter (a letter that introduces you and your business to a potential strategic partner who might be able to refer customers to you). Send this letter to one potential strategic partner each month.

Here's how a prospect and customer might go through that system:

1. I love horses and have been considering taking riding lessons for months now, but with all the riding stables out there, I don't know which to choose. I'm on Facebook and I notice an ad (KNOW) at the side of the page promoting an eBook on how to choose the best riding instructor for you.

2. I click on the link and come to a landing page. Since I've been having trouble deciding on a riding instructor and stable, I'm really interesting in knowing what to look for. I enter my email address and receive the eBook (TRY).

3. The eBook outlines some great points, so I click through to the company's website to find out more about them. I read their story on their

about page, and they seem like really nice people (LIKE). I also notice a case study from a previous customer who was in the same situation as me. These are the exact results I am hoping to get! (TRUST)

4. I decide to take the leap – I sign up for a set of three lessons on the website. I immediately receive an email confirmation along with a customer welcome kit I can download. The welcome kit tells me what to expect at my first lesson, who my instructor will be, and what to bring and wear. This makes me feel like these people know what they're doing and have a clear process in place. Even better, they included a bonus 30 minute horsemanship session. I didn't expect that! Now I really feel like I made the right decision.

5. I'm so excited about my free session that I post about my experience on my Facebook horse group. Ten of my friends like the post and three of them say they're going to check out the stable too.

6. I've completed my first two riding lessons and everything is going well. I get home from my lesson and find a newsletter from the riding stable in my email. I open it up and read it

immediately. How interesting – I didn't know they also offered an evening group for women to get together, drink wine, and learn more about horses. It's only $30 a month, so I sign up for that too. (REPEAT)

7. I really like my riding lessons and women's horse group, so it's time to get some real horseback riding boots and clothes. I head to the local tack store and while I'm there, I see a form at the front to get 10% off riding lessons at my stable. I didn't know the tack shop knew them. I talk to the lady at the front desk, and she told me they got a letter from the stable a while back, and since they share the same core horsemanship beliefs, they now refer customers to each other. It's a great relationship. (REFER)

So hopefully by now you know:

- The types of thought leadership content and tactics you can choose from
- How to organize your content and tactics using the Marketing Hourglass
- How to turn the elements in your Marketing Hourglass into a Thought Leadership System
- How this Thought Leadership System might work in the real world

But now you're asking yourself, what types of content, tactics, and distribution methods would a typical business use?

After all, you likely (ok more than likely) won't be using all of the tactics and delivery methods listed. We just wanted to show you the breadth of options available. You will need to choose the tactics and distribution methods that work best for you.

The level and frequency of your written content publishing/distribution or speaking will also depend on your budget. We understand that most small businesses will not be able to budget in all of these tactics at the highest level and frequency, and that is A-OK. Let this list give you some ideas of where you can start now, and help you set future goals for your thought leadership content distribution.

Below are some real-life examples of how three very different businesses developed their thought leadership systems. The following content publishing/distribution schedules were prepared as reasonable schedules and budgets to work with for each of the various types of businesses.

Example 1: B2B Mid-Size Company – Software for Corporations and Higher Education

After three years, Acme Software is no longer a start-up and has decided it needs to get serious about its marketing program. The company has a marketing budget, but it needs to be a lot smarter about how it uses and tracks the budget. The company also needs to create some systems around marketing as it prepares to grow.

Acme Software's Do Leadership Program:

Year One:

1. Four blog posts per month (one per week)
   a. Post on the company website
   b. Share on social media
   c. Include some in the monthly company newsletter
2. Monthly newsletter
   a. Send to customers and prospects via email
3. Press releases, bi-monthly
   a. Pay for distribution via an industry appropriate organization
   b. Post to the "In the News" section on the company website
   c. Share via social media and in the monthly newsletter
4. Quarterly webinar
   a. Post on the website
   b. Publish in the monthly newsletter

c.   Have strategic partners publish in their newsletters

5. Quarterly case study
    a. Post on the website
    b. Publish in the monthly newsletter
    c. Share with strategic partners

6. Sponsored content
    a.   Twice a year, sponsor an industry guide where the company thought leader comments on an industry question and then publish the comment as an editorial in the guide
    b.   Share in a blog post on the company website
    c.   Publish in the monthly newsletter
    d.   Publish on LinkedIn and other social channels

7. Annual industry conferences
    a.   Attend and be a speaker for at least one industry conference
    b.   Post presentation to website
    c.   Post presentation to Slideshare
    d.   Share on social media and in the newsletter

By the end of the first year, Acme Software will have the following:

1.   More than 200 shares of content on social media
2.   70 permanent content assets working for the company on an ongoing basis:
    • 70 new pages on the website
    • 52 new blog posts

- 6 news releases
- 4 case studies
- 4 webinars
- 12 newsletters
- 2 pieces of sponsored content
- 1 industry presentation

Each piece of content can rank independently on Google, which will assist with the company's search engine optimization efforts. Also, having content on external sources such as industry websites and sites like Slideshare will assist in generating authority and credibility on and offline.

While there are some more advanced marketing activities in this example, it is possible to accomplish all of this with the help of a marketing agency as opposed to hiring a full-time employee.

Example 2 – Small B2C Online Pet Supplies

Abby's Pet Supplies is an online pet supply retailer. Abby has been in the business for about five years and has been marketing all along. However, her marketing efforts have always been rather random, and Abby now wants to take it to the next level.

Abby's Pet Supplies Do Leadership Program:

Year One:

1. Daily posts to social media
   a. Product pictures
   b. Favorite pet photos
2. Two blog posts per week
   - One post is written content and one post is a video; both will go on the company website
   - Share on social media
   - Include in monthly company newsletter
3. Monthly newsletter
   a. Send to customers and prospects via email
4. Quarterly virtual event
   a. Virtual how-to presentation and annual pet gift giving event
   b. Post presentation to website
   c. Post presentation to Slideshare
   d. Share via social media and in the newsletter

By the end of the first year, Abby's Pet Supplies will have the following:

1. Hundreds of social shares on social media and via email
2. 104 permanent content assets working for the company on an ongoing basis:
   a. 104 new web pages with written and video content

> b. 4 new virtual events recorded and posted on the website for ongoing viewing

For Abby, just getting consistent with her marketing will help tremendously with her online search results. The virtual events and video blogging help differentiate her from the competition.

Example 3: Solopreneur – Life Coach

Lisa just completed a life coaching program. She has made a deal with her current full-time job to go down to part time hours while she completes her program. In the meantime, she is setting up and launching her new business. She doesn't have a lot of time or a large budget.

Lisa's Do Leadership Program:

Year One:

1. Two blog posts per month
   a. Post on her website
   b. Share on social media
2. One newsletter per quarter
   a. Send to prospects/customers via email
   b. Create a web page and add to the current and past newsletters section on her website
   c. Share on social media
3. Two news releases a year

     a.   Post to the news release section on her website

     b.   Post to a free PR website, PRBuzz.com

     c.   Share via social media and in the newsletter

4. Social Media:

     a.   Post four additional social media posts per week

In terms of time and effort, Lisa would be spending time on marketing twice a month, or about 8 hours.

With this minimal thought leadership program, by the end of the first year Lisa will have the following:

1. About 200 shares of content on social media and via email

2. 20 permanent content assets working for her on an ongoing basis:

- 20 new web pages on Lisa's website answering key customer questions, including:
    - 12 blog posts
    - Two news releases
    - One article
    - Two webinars
    - Three newsletters
- Each piece of content above will rank independently on Google, which means that when prospects are searching for answers to

their questions, Lisa's blog posts may come up.

- Additionally, one article and two news releases will be posted to additional areas of the internet where prospects can find them.

Year Two:

In year two, Lisa had her blogs, newsletters, and news releases down to a nice system and found she had some more free time to spend on marketing – so she added a few more activities:

1. One article per year
   a. Post to the articles section on the website
   b. Post to an online article site
   c. Share on social media and in the newsletter
2. One webinar per year
   a. Record live, then post on the website
   b. Send to customers via email
   c. Share on social media and in the newsletter
3. One speaking session per year
   a. Post to SlideShare
   b. Share on social media and in the newsletter

Want to know a little secret? For almost every single item you've just read, there are infinite possibilities for repurposing the content. It's like slicing and dicing to turn one meal into many. For example, nearly every other item on the list will produce the sort of content you could use on your blog.

Keep repurposing in mind as you create content to use in your thought leadership strategy, and you'll save yourself a lot of work. It takes a lot more effort and resources to create a hundred different pieces of content than it does to create just a few and repurpose them a hundred different ways. By repurposing, not only are your efforts more efficient, your story is more unified as you share content with your customers. People don't remember much of what they read, watch, or hear – so don't worry about them noticing that you've repurposed some of your content. Most likely, they won't even notice – but if they do, there's a good chance they'll feel more connected to your brand because they know that particular part of your story already.

It's important to remember that as a business owner, we are immersed in our company and see our message over and over, so it's easy to start thinking that we're overwhelming or irritating our customers with the same message. Not true – the reality is that your company is not the only thing your audience pays attention to, so the likelihood of exhausting anyone other than you and your employees with your message is minimal. In fact, the opposite is the danger – your audience typically needs to see a message seven times before it starts to sink in. Seven times. That's a lot.

Especially considering that the moment your blog posted, members of your audience could have run to the bathroom, grabbed a coffee, or been focused on their own work.

The real risk is not sharing your message enough.

> *Thought leaders have to understand that the reason why you need to be yourself and say things in your own words is that there are people out there who will get the idea because you're saying it, and they won't get it if somebody else says it.*
>
> **Thomas Sterner, Author of** *The Practicing Mind*

Thought Leadership System for Creation and Delivery

Once you've selected your tactics and distribution methods, you need to determine how to deliver your tactics, who will deliver them, and what tools you will use. This becomes your Thought Leadership System – and when you can clearly identify each step of the system and who will be responsible for each step, you will find that your system becomes streamlined and extremely effective.

Just for an example, a Thought Leadership System might look like this:

1. CEO drafts a blog post.

2. Marketing manager edits the blog post.

3. Marketing coordinator posts the blog.

4. Once the blog post is on the website, the marketing coordinator uses a social media management system to distribute the post to whichever social channels are deemed appropriate, such as:

   - LinkedIn

   - Facebook

   - Twitter

It's easy to see the importance of having the right people in place to delegate the tasks of your system. If you don't have the right people on staff to do this, you can hire a contractor to do it for you. And even if you have one person handling multiple tasks, it's fine – as long as each person knows his or her task and responsibility and completes it correctly and on time. The thought leadership calendar will also help keep everyone on task and stick to the steps of the system.

The biggest thing you have to do, and this is hard, you have to have a real point of view. It doesn't have to be earth shattering. If you want to become a thought leader you've got to have some unique twist or point of view that might be contrary and you have to own it.

John Jantsch, Founder of Duct Tape Marketing

Secret to Success: Thought Leadership Calendar

The secret to becoming a thought leader is to deliver your thoughts or content on a routine and consistent basis. If you publish new content only once in a while, you won't be considered a serious thought leader. Create a calendar that outlines your content themes, and the type of content you will be creating and delivering:

- Daily
- Weekly
- Monthly
- Quarterly
- Annually

When it comes to your thought leadership calendar, get as specific as you can. As we discussed in Chapter 5, you will want to weave your thought leadership themes into every piece of content you create. For your calendar, you can determine when to share what, and who will do the tasks. It ALL goes on the calendar, so there are no questions as to what is happening from week to week.

Being organized in this way will save you an incredible amount of time and keep everyone on the same page … er, calendar. You won't have to have multiple email discussions … or (gasp!) dreaded staff meetings about what you should publish on the blog this week or what the topic should be on your upcoming podcast – it's already on the calendar. No one is scrambling to figure it out. You will be running your system like a well-oiled machine. Simple!

Using a calendar ensures that everyone performs their content creation duties on a consistent, routine basis. Doing this will get you results, and results are the key to success.

To assist you with this, we've created a sample Marketing Calendar or marketing routine to help you understand what this might look like. You can access this sample marketing calendar at this link:

When you can begin to publish content on a regular basis, you will attract a following of readers and listeners who develop expectations for your content. They'll look for your updates and news because it becomes part of their media usage habit. What could be better for business than becoming a part of your prospects' lives in such a way? You become like a friend – they feel like they know you, and you become a trusted source of reliable information.

BOOM! Thought leadership jackpot!

Now that you have an understanding of the three steps to becoming a thought leader, your mind is probably scrambling to fit this new concept into your overall plan for marketing. You're about to be pleasantly surprised by how neatly it will fit.

Your first intention can't be about making money. It has to be about helping. Whenever we doubt what we're doing, we go back to focusing on helping people. You have to write and have an online presence, those two in combination are really important. Being a mentor to your audience, you have to build trust, and this doesn't happen overnight. Build relationships with leaders in your industry. Be authentic, not a copycat. Have enough confidence to put yourself out there, participate and be in front of people, even if it takes you outside your comfort zone.

Jean Hanson, Co-founder at The Janitorial Store

CHAPTER 8

NEXT STEPS

Congratulations! You've reached the end of the book, and should have a pretty good idea of what thought leadership is, why it's important, and the steps you need to take to "Do Thought Leadership" for your business.

Download Your Free Do Leadership Plan Template Now:

If you haven't already, it's time to download your Do Leadership Plan Template and two bonus Thought Leadership Calendar templates.

http://ducttapepublishing.com/book/do-leadership/

Follow the steps in the template (remember – they match the three steps we've gone through in this book) to map out your Do Leadership Plan and then create your annual thought leadership calendar.

Download here:
www.DuctTapePublishing.com/do-leadership-resources

Need More Support?

If you need more support, we're here to help. The following pages include details about each of the authors of this book and how to contact them if you'd like more information.

ABOUT THE AUTHORS

Duct Tape Marketing consultants know busy. It's their busy business owner or solopreneur clients more than any others who simultaneously need and yet are often baffled by one of the most powerful results-producing strategies ever to hit the world of commerce: thought leadership.

The mixed feelings of optimistic enthusiasm and utter overwhelmed-ness most business owners have when they think about leveraging thought leadership to generate highly-qualified, eager prospects is why you're holding this book right now. Thought leadership seems too lofty, too cerebral, too costly a tool for small- and mid-sized businesses to wield. After all, when was the last time you got paid to sit and think great thoughts, anyway? And yet, it makes perfect sense – people want to do business with an expert they feel connected to somehow, who has held their hand and given them the information they need all along the way.

Duct Tape Marketing is nothing if not practical – and that's what these acclaimed marketing consultants have created with this guide. Forget about being just a "thought" leader and engage in DO leadership instead. (Spoiler Alert: You're probably already halfway there and don't even know it!)

In *Do Leadership*, Nicole Croizier, Laura P. Lorenz, Ray L. Perry, and Kelly Weppler Hernandez join forces to strip the mystique out of this dynamo of a marketing strategy and put it within reach of a business of any size. In this quick and easy read, you'll get the kind of complete recipe for success any business owner can follow, starting today.

Nicole Croizier
www.lovewhatyoudoagain.com
nicole@corneryourmarket.ca

Nicole Croizier is both a Master Certified Duct Tape Marketing Consultant and Endorsed Soul's Calling Coach. She combines her expertise in marketing with life and equus coaching to help frustrated coaches, solopreneurs and small business owners with soul love what they do again.

Nicole's background includes a degree in Communication from Simon Fraser University, and 16 years as a corporate marketing executive in the B2B and high technology world. Her background ranges from launching start-up companies and acting as a one-woman marketing department to leading marketing teams for large software firms and managing a $15 million brand.

In 2011, Nicole left the corporate world to found solopreneur firm Corner Your Market. She partnered with the leading small business marketing brand Duct Tape Marketing in 2012, and HubSpot Inbound Marketing in 2013.

Since 2012, Nicole has supported solopreneurs and small business owners in better understanding, communicating and marketing their businesses by taking a strategy-first approach to marketing and installing powerful and practical marketing and thought leadership systems.

Today, Nicole combines her expertise in marketing with life and equus coaching to help frustrated coaches, solopreneurs and small business owners connect who they are to businesses and marketing systems they love. She teaches business & marketing classes for the Martha Beck Wayfinder Coach Training Program, and partners with the Soul's Calling Academy to deliver coach training, intensive retreats and courses.

If you're a solopreneur or entrepreneur with soul, and looking for a way to find your soul's niche, design a business you love, and market your business in a way that is authentic, non-salesy and fun – then visit www.lovewhatyoudoagain.com

Laura B. Lorenz
www.leadingresults.com
llorenz@leadingresults.com

Laura B. Lorenz' passion has always been to help organizations reach their goals.

Whether helping build a marketing agency, working as a sales and marketing coach with small technology companies selling Great Plains Software or as a consultant developing fundraising strategies with foundations and organizations, Laura has been in the trenches working as a team member, hand in hand, to develop and implement strategies that drive results.

She brings her expertise to the forefront in the development and execution of:
- Marketing planning – pragmatic and practical strategies that are affordable and able to be implemented with the resources available.
- Strategic thinking – cross-industry experience that allows for the introduction of effective programs and strategies to new markets
- Sales 2.0 - The integration of the sales and marketing processes in logical and meaningful ways
- Marketing tactics – dynamic interpersonal skills that drive accountable results.

Laura's affiliation the Duct Tape Marketing system gives her a platform to effectively leverage her passions and expertise. Most businesses begin and end using marketing tactics void of a planned strategy. Laura's client engagements clearly demonstrate her ability put strategy before tactics in order to drive effective results. For example, she has:

- Collaboratively built marketing and business kickoff plan for a technology start up that allowed for consistent year-over-year growth for 5+ years
- Created focus on helping more than 100 businesses refine their overall business strategy to focus on their profitable core competencies
- Coached client's executives to focus on their core business competencies, enabling them to clearly see improved processes and results through delegation to current and new staff

She is a high energy, accomplished facilitator on small business marketing strategies, speaker, and author. With over 30 years experience in marketing and sales coaching, she understands the importance of having the right strategies and tools to grow a small business.

Laura's strong appetite for learning has allowed her to say on top of the latest tools and techniques. She combines her many years of experience with the ever-evolving world of social marketing to help her clients achieve their objectives.

Co-author of Do Leadership: A Step by Step Guide to "Doing" Thought Leadership for Solopreneurs & Small Business Owners

Personal: Laura lives in Stony Point NC with husband Ken and too many pets! She loves gardening, enjoying all things on the lake, and has been known to scuba dive and skydive.

For more information about Laura, visit:
www.leadingresults.com
llorenz@leadingresults.com
Phone: 610-883-2230

Ray L. Perry
Owner of MarketBlazer, Inc.
www.MarketBlazer.com

Ray L. Perry is a marketing consultant, business advisor and author of Guide to Marketing Your Business Online (2011) and co-author of:

- *Renewable Referrals: How to Cultivate More Profits* (2014)
- *The Small Business Owners Guide to Local Lead Generation: Proven Strategies & Tips to Grow Your Business* (2015)
- *Do Leadership: A Step-by-Step Guide to Doing Thought Leadership* (2016)
- *Content Marketing for Local Search: Create Content that Google Loves & Prospects Devour* (2019)
- *Avid Strategy: How Focus, Culture and Commitment Can Grow Your Small Business* (coming soon)
- *Marketing Guides for Small Business eBooks: Local SEO, Google AdWords and Reputation Management.*

Ray is also a featured author on Duct Tape Publishing. To learn more about Ray's books visit: www.amazon.com/author/rayperry.

Ray is the founder and Chief Marketing Officer at MarketBlazer, Inc., a technology-based marketing agency specializing in small business lead generation, lead conversion, and customer engagement. Ray brings to the MarketBlazer team nearly three decades of leadership expertise in operations, sales, and marketing of technology products and services within start-up and high-growth entrepreneurial environments, plus C level management experience. Ray understands the marketing process and its role in supporting the growth of small businesses.

MarketBlazer combines their unique 7-step marketing framework and strong technology expertise with the latest marketing tactics, including online marketing, content marketing and social media marketing to develop solid long-term inbound marketing strategies for clients. The MarketBlazer goal with marketing is simple and straight forward; **To help your business thrive.** To learn more about improving your small business marketing visit www.MarketBlazer.com

Ray is a Master Marketing Consultant certified by Duct Tape Marketing, specializing in developing a unique marketing strategy focused on your ideal customers and designed to set your business apart from your competitors. Ray is a StoryBrand Certified Guide, specializing in developing engaging content to improve your messaging and tell your unique story. Additionally, Ray is a Customer Value Optimization Specialist certified by Digital Marketer, specializing in developing optimized sales funnels for generating higher quality leads at a lower acquisition cost. To learn more visit www.raylperry.com

Bonus Offer: Get a professional Marketing Strategy Audit today. Normally $299, for a limited time this valuable one-on-one consultation is only $99. To learn more visit www.MarketingStrategyAudit.com.

Follow Ray L. Perry:
www.twitter.com/raylperry
www.linkedin.com/in/raylperry

Learn More about Ray's Books:
www.amazon.com/author/rayperry
www.raylperry.com

Special Offers from Ray:
Free SEO Analysis
Do you realize how not having the right SEO on your small business website could be preventing your ideal customers from connecting with you? Make sure you are getting it right; your business success literally depends upon it! Fill out a simple form by following the link below to get a professional SEO analysis that will ensure you are doing it right and setting up your business for success online.
www.marketblazer.com/resources/seo-analysis/

Small Business Marketing Training
Don't get left behind in the game of marketing for your small business! Access the small business marketing training that will help you compete in your local niche. Wherever you are today, no matter how small or disorganized your marketing plan may be   you can become the #1 player in your niche when you have the right strategy in place. Free library of valuable marketing eBooks by John Jantsch, founder of Duct Tape Marketing and Ray L. Perry, chief marketing officer of MarketBlazer. Follow the link below.
www.needmarketing.com

Kelly Weppler Hernandez
WH & Associates, Marketing
Strategists
www.whandassociates.com
kelly@whandassociates.com
Phone: 949-633-6341

Kelly Weppler Hernandez is a marketing strategist who focuses on awareness and lead generation for small B2B technology companies. Kelly is instrumental in developing strategic partnerships and has taken businesses from start-up to a global presence.

After working with clients to build the strategy, she assists them with executing a tactical marketing action plan that combines high tech with high touch to deliver success. She says the technology is necessary to scale processes and track efforts, but the personal touch is vital in building a business people will remember.

Kelly has been interviewed by the American Marketing Association, written for several entrepreneurial and small business magazines and online resources, and co-wrote a book called *Renewable Referrals—How To Cultivate More Profits.*

Kelly is a Master Duct Tape Marketing Consultant and the founder of WH & Associates, a marketing coaching and consulting firm in Orange County, California.

For more information about Kelly, visit:
www.whandassociates.com.